A Guide to
AMERICAN STATES

Vermont

THE GREEN MOUNTAIN STATE

www.av2books.com

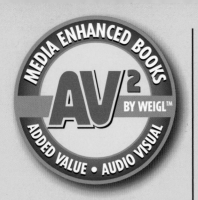

AV² provides enriched content that supplements and complements this book. Weigl's AV² books strive to create inspired learning and engage young minds in a total learning experience.

Your AV² Media Enhanced books come alive with...

Audio
Listen to sections of the book read aloud.

Key Words
Study vocabulary, and complete a matching word activity.

Video
Watch informative video clips.

Quizzes
Test your knowledge.

Embedded Weblinks
Gain additional information for research.

Slide Show
View images and captions, and prepare a presentation.

**Go to www.av2books.com,
and enter this book's
unique code.**

BOOK CODE

Z 4 2 0 6 2 1

AV² by Weigl brings you media enhanced books that support active learning.

Try This!
Complete activities and hands-on experiments.

... and much, much more!

Published by AV² by Weigl
350 5ᵗʰ Avenue, 59ᵗʰ Floor
New York, NY 10118
Website: www.av2books.com   www.weigl.com

Library of Congress Cataloging-in-Publication Data

Foran, Jill.
  Vermont / Jill Foran.
    p. cm. -- (A guide to American states)
  Includes index.
  ISBN 978-1-61690-818-8 (hardcover : alk. paper) -- ISBN 978-1-61690-494-4 (online)
  1. Vermont--Juvenile literature. I. Title.
  F49.3.F663 2011
  974.3--dc23
                         2011019235

Printed in the United States of America in North Mankato, Minnesota

052011
WEP180511

Project Coordinator Jordan McGill
Art Director Terry Paulhus

Photo Credits
Every reasonable effort has been made to trace ownership and to obtain permission to reprint copyright material. The publishers would be pleased to have any errors or omissions brought to their attention so that they may be corrected in subsequent printings.

Weigl acknowledges Getty Images as its primary image supplier for this title.

Contents

Woodstock, first settled in 1768, was named after a town in England. This beautiful historic village is located in southeastern Vermont.

Introduction

T he saying "good things come in small packages" describes the state of Vermont. In addition to being one of the smallest states in the country, Vermont is also one of the least populous. At its widest point Vermont is less than 90 miles from east to west, and from north to south, it is only about 160 miles long. Despite its small size, the state is rich in history, culture, and natural beauty.

Vermont joined the Union in 1791, making it the first state to do so after the original 13 colonies. The state's earliest European settlers were of British heritage. Today Vermont is populated largely by offspring of the original settlers and of later immigrants from Great Britain, Ireland, Italy, Poland, Canada, and other nations. Some residents of French Canadian heritage speak French at home.

Vermont has many black-and-white cows, called Holsteins. They weigh an average of about 1,500 pounds.

Expert skiers and snowboarders from around the world travel to Stowe to conquer its challenging runs.

Most of Vermont's residents live in small villages and towns. Vermonters are known for their independence, and the state's residents value the peace and quiet that rural life has to offer. Small towns tend to differ from big cities. For instance, town centers are usually quieter and less smoggy than city centers. Even Vermont's urban centers are small. Residents treasure the unspoiled land, and many make efforts to preserve their environment.

Many visitors are drawn to Vermont by the state's impressive natural beauty. The greatest draws are the excellent ski resorts, especially in the Green Mountains. The state has more than 5,000 acres of hills, ranging from gentle to extreme slopes. Many of these hills are used for skiing or snowboarding. Stowe, which receives about 260 inches of snowfall every year, is a very popular ski destination. It is also the location of Mount Mansfield, the highest mountain in the state.

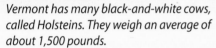

Where Is Vermont?

Vermont is located in the northeast corner of the United States and is part of the New England region. Of all the New England states, Vermont is the only one that does not have an Atlantic Ocean coastline.

There are many ways to get to Vermont. Interstate highways provide easy access to most of the state's cities and towns. For those arriving by air, there are many small public airports. The largest and busiest airport in Vermont is the Burlington International Airport. Lake Champlain is also a popular transportation route.

Ferryboats transport passengers and cars across Lake Champlain in all seasons.

The name Vermont has connections to the state's history and landscape. Vermont comes from the French words *vert*, which means "green," and *mont*, which means "mountain."

The Green Mountains run down the center of the state and cover most of the land. These heavily forested highlands are part of the Appalachian Mountains. They give Vermont its nickname, the Green Mountain State.

The Green Mountain National Forest contains Moss Glen Falls. These dramatic falls have a total drop of 125 feet.

Mapping
Vermont

Vermont is bordered on the north by the Canadian province of Quebec and on the south by Massachusetts. To the west is New York, which is separated from Vermont for about 100 miles by Lake Champlain. The Connecticut River forms Vermont's border with New Hampshire on the east.

Sites and Symbols

STATE SEAL
Vermont

STATE BIRD
Hermit Thrush

STATE FLOWER
Red Clover

STATE FLAG
Vermont

STATE ANIMAL
Morgan Horse

STATE TREE
Maple

Nickname The Green Mountain State

Motto Freedom and Unity

Song "These Green Mountains," words and music by Diane Martin

Entered the Union March 4, 1791, as the 14th state

Capital Montpelier

Population (2010 Census) 625,741 Ranked 49th state

Map Scale

0   100 Miles

N

QUEBEC

Rouses Point
Swanton
Newport
Derby Line
Colebrook
Plattsburgh
St. Albans
Orleans
Milton
Cambridge
Groveton
Keeseville
Morrisville
Hardwick
Lyndonville
Lancaster
Jericho
Burlington
St. Johnsbury
Gorham
Richmond
Cabot
Whitefield
Marshfield
Littleton

NEW YORK

Elizabethtown

Montpelier
Barre
Vergennes
Northfield
Graniteville
Wells River
Bristol
VERMONT
North Conway
Conway

Port Henry
Middlebury
Bradford

NEW HAMPSHIRE

Ticonderoga
Randolph
Brandon
Bethel
Plymouth
Ashland
Pittsford
Hanover
Lebanon
Warrensburg
Woodstock
Whitehall
Rutland
Franklin
Laconia
Glens Falls
Wallingford
New London
Fernwood
Claremont
Fort Edward
Springfield
Saratoga Springs
Henniker
Country Knolls
Manchester Center
Bellows Falls
Hillsborough
Antrim
Schenectady
Arlington
Keene
Peterborough
Troy
Bennington
Brattleboro
Jaffrey
Albany
Readsboro
Williamstown
Winchenden
Nassau
MASSACHUSETTS Athol
Greenfield

LEGEND
— Road
— River
⭐ State Capital
• City
▦ Vermont
— State Border

STATE CAPITAL

Montpelier has been the capital of Vermont since 1805. The city is named for Montpellier, France. With only about 7,800 residents, Montpelier is one of the least populous state capitals in the United States.

United States

Hawai'i Alaska

Vermont

The Land

Vermont offers spectacular landscapes. The average altitude in the state is 1,000 feet. The Green Mountains run through central Vermont. On the border with Massachusetts, the northern end of the Hoosac Range enters Vermont, and the Taconic Range rises along the southwestern side. The Taconic Range contains Mount Equinox, which rises to 3,816 feet. The name Taconic is thought to have come from an Algonquian Indian word referring to a tree, a wood, or a forest. Many of the mountain areas are covered with forest. Only about one-sixth of the land is level with fertile soil. Most of this land is in the Champlain Valley, which borders Lake Champlain.

QUECHEE GORGE

On the Ottauquechee River is Vermont's deepest gorge. The movement of **glaciers** more than 10,000 years ago formed this narrow, steep-walled canyon in Hartford. Quechee Gorge is 1 mile long and 165 feet deep.

GREEN MOUNTAINS

Green Mountain National Forest, established in 1932, covers nearly 400,000 acres of scenic woodlands and mountains.

MOUNT MANSFIELD

Vermont has 223 mountains with elevations above 2,000 feet. The tallest is Mount Mansfield, which rises to 4,393 feet in the Green Mountains area.

LAKE CHAMPLAIN

Lake Champlain, at 95 feet above sea level, is the state's lowest point. Lake Champlain is the sixth-largest body of freshwater in the United States.

Vermont's Long Trail served as the inspiration for the Appalachian Trail, a long-distance hiking trail that runs for about 2,175 miles from Maine to Georgia. The Appalachian Trail overlaps the Long Trail for about 100 miles in the southern part of Vermont.

Environmental conservation is in full force at Vermont's ski areas. From recycling to energy conservation, Vermonters work to preserve the environment and maintain the state's natural beauty.

Vermont's major rivers include the Connecticut, Missisquoi, Lamoille, Winooski, White, Battenkill, and West rivers, as well as Otter Creek.

Vermont has numerous state forests, the largest of which is the nearly 40,000-acre Mount Mansfield State Forest.

Vermont experiences frequent snowstorms during the winter months.

Climate

T he mountains and valleys of Vermont are usually blanketed in snow for at least five months every year. Winter temperatures can drop below –34° Fahrenheit. The state's lowest recorded temperature was –50° F in Bloomfield on December 30, 1933. The state's winters are generally long and cold.

Vermont summers are short and cool. Summer evening temperatures drop quickly, especially in the mountains. In summer, temperatures rarely rise above 90° F. The highest temperature ever recorded in Vermont was 105° F on July 4, 1911, in Vernon.

Average Temperatures Across Vermont

Average annual temperatures in many towns and cities across Vermont are a little above 45° F. Why might Jay Peak have a colder average annual temperature?

Degrees Fahrenheit

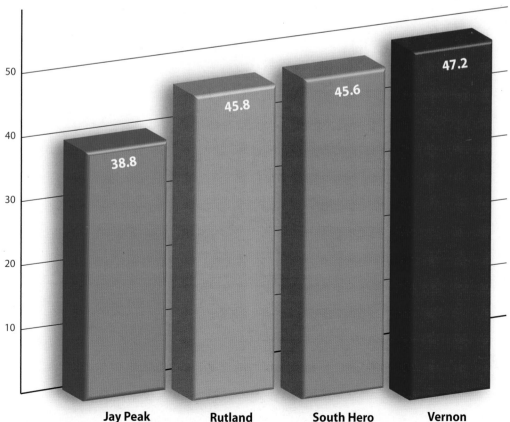

Jay Peak	Rutland	South Hero	Vernon
38.8	45.8	45.6	47.2

Natural Resources

A lthough Vermont is small, it has a wealth of natural resources. These include dense forests and valuable mineral and rock deposits. The state's principal mining location is the Green Mountains region. Granite is the leading mined product. In fact, the largest granite **quarries** in the United States, and some of the largest in the world, are located around Barre. Vermont also produces sand, gravel, talc, gemstones, slate, and limestone.

The Rock of Ages quarry, founded in Graniteville in 1885, sits on top of a deposit of granite 10 miles deep.

With about three-fourths of its land covered by forests, Vermont counts trees among its important natural resources. Lumber and plywood are the leading wood products. Other wood products include hockey sticks, furniture, and paper.

Vermont syrup producers begin to collect sap from maple trees in early spring. This time is known as "the sugaring season," when sap begins to flow. Syrup producers drive a metal spout into one or more holes in each tree. A bucket is hung from each spout to collect sap. Buckets are emptied into a large barrel, which is taken to a building called a sugarhouse. The sap is then boiled until pure maple syrup remains.

Maple syrup may also be obtained through the modern pipeline system. The sap runs through tubes that are connected to the spouts and is drained into a pipeline that connects to the sugarhouse. This method requires less time and labor.

Vermont is the leading producer of maple syrup in the United States.

Plants

Though much of Vermont is now forested, the state had few woodlands as recently as 150 years ago because settlers had cleared most of the land for agriculture. Since the mid-1800s Vermonters have worked hard to replant and maintain their forests. Most of the trees that dominate the Vermont landscape today are **deciduous**, including maple, elm, birch, oak, and cherry. Each fall the leaves on these trees change color, displaying shades of vivid red, purple, orange, and gold. **Conifers**, which are commonly found in Vermont's mountain areas, include white pines, hemlocks, and cedars.

Other types of plant life also flourish in Vermont. The most common wildflowers that decorate the state are buttercups, goldenrods, daisies, violets, and lilacs.

WHITE PINE TREE

White pine trees are the tallest in eastern North America, growing to more than 100 feet tall. These hardy, valuable trees can live hundreds of years.

SUGAR MAPLE TREE

Vermont's state tree is the sugar maple. The sap of this tree supports the maple syrup industry. The wood is used to make furniture, flooring, and musical instruments. Sugar maples, known for their colorful fall foliage, can reach heights of 100 feet.

LADY'S SLIPPERS

Lady's slippers belong to the orchid family. These showy wildflowers are usually whitish pink, and they bloom from May to July.

RED CLOVERS

Red clover is Vermont's state flower. Used as animal feed, it is also beneficial to farmland. Clover adds valuable **nitrogen** to the soil and increases the availability of other nutrients for certain crops.

Autumn in Vermont is known as the foliage season. It usually begins in mid-September and continues into October. The leaves of trees change color in autumn because of a decrease in the production of the green pigment called chlorophyll. This allows other colors in the leaves to show through.

Vermont is a leader in environmental awareness. In 1970 it passed the Environmental Control Law, which allows the government to restrict development that might harm the environment.

About 85 percent of Vermont's forestland is privately owned.

Animals

Vermont's forests are home to a variety of animals. White-tailed deer are common throughout many of the state's wooded areas. Larger animals, such as bears, moose, and bobcats, live in the higher mountain regions. Other common animals found in the state include skunks, raccoons, minks, rabbits, squirrels, and woodchucks.

Various waterfowl can be found bobbing on Vermont's lakes. Ducks, loons, and Canada geese are just a few of the birds that visit the area. The quiet waters and wetlands of Missisquoi National Wildlife Refuge attract large flocks of **migratory** birds. This refuge is located on the eastern shore of Lake Champlain and provides about 6,500 acres of protected animal habitat. Beavers, bullfrogs, snapping turtles, and otters also live in Vermont's wetland areas.

EASTERN CHIPMUNK

Eastern chipmunks are abundant throughout Vermont. Most of their time is spent searching for and feeding on plants and other animals. Inner cheek pouches help them store and transport their food.

EASTERN BLUEBIRD

The eastern bluebird has a royal blue back and head with a red-brown breast. Its wings are long, but the tail is short. These songbirds are most common in pastures, backyards, and golf courses.

LUNA MOTH

This pale green moth lives in hardwood forests in eastern North America. Its wingspan measures about four inches. Before it becomes a moth, it feeds on leaves and spins a silky cocoon.

RIVER OTTER

Otters are members of the weasel family. These playful animals are expert swimmers and divers, and they can remain underwater for three or four minutes. They live close to water, moving awkwardly on land.

More than 300 species of birds are found in Vermont. The state bird is the hermit thrush.

About 60 species of mammals, including many different types of bats, inhabit Vermont.

The honeybee is Vermont's official insect. This insect produces honey for the state's beekeepers and helps pollinate crops for local farmers.

Vermont has many raccoons. Raccoons live on the ground and in trees. They usually hunt for food at night and stay in their dens during the day.

Tourism

Every year more than 4 million people visit the Green Mountain State. Vermont's beautiful scenery and many recreational opportunities make it a popular year-round vacation spot. In the fall, tourists travel to the state to see the spectacular colors of the trees. During the winter, visitors go to Vermont to enjoy its first-rate ski facilities. Springtime takes people to the state for the maple syrup harvest, where they watch this sweet, sticky liquid being made. In the summer, tourists take pleasure in outdoor activities such as hiking, fishing, and camping.

Vermont contains many historical attractions. The Vermont Historical Society Museum, in Montpelier, traces the history of the state since the time of its earliest European settlers, who arrived in the 1600s.

TRAPP FAMILY LODGE

In 1939, the Trapp family, portrayed in the film *The Sound of Music*, moved to Stowe, a tiny mountain town that reminded them of their homeland in Austria. Founded in 1950, the Trapp Family Lodge now offers lodging, restaurants, a bakery, and 2,400 acres of natural areas.

ECHO LAKE AQUARIUM AND SCIENCE CENTER

This Burlington aquarium has more than 70 species of live animals, some 100 interactive experiences, and a 7,000-gallon lake tank. The waterfront center gets about 100,000 visitors a year.

SHELBURNE MUSEUM

Founded in 1947, this sprawling museum includes a historic railroad station, lighthouse, and covered bridge. A 220-foot steamship is also on the grounds. The museum houses early American folk art, quilts, furniture, and a carved wooden figurehead from the bow of a late-19th-century American ship.

SHELBURNE FARMS

Shelburne Farms, a National Historic Landmark, is a 1,400-acre working farm on the shores of Lake Champlain. Visitors enjoy the walking trails, tours of the grounds, and children's farmyard.

I DIDN'T KNOW THAT!

The Old Constitution House, in Windsor, is the site where Vermont's first constitution was adopted in 1777. At that time, the building was a tavern.

The Bennington Battle Monument commemorates the Battle of Bennington, fought on August 16, 1777, during the American Revolution. At more than 300 feet high, it is Vermont's tallest structure. Visitors can ride an elevator to the top for views of Vermont, Massachusetts, and New York.

Snowmobiling is a popular sport in Vermont. Thousands of miles of trails are groomed throughout the state.

Industry

I ndustry in Vermont has undergone major changes. **Textile** mills used to be very important in the state, but most of the firms have closed or moved to the South or overseas.

Manufacturing remains an important economic activity in the state of Vermont. The state's manufacturing now focuses on more modern industries, however.

Industries in Vermont
Value of Goods and Services in Millions of Dollars

Generating more than $5 billion a year, finance, insurance, and real estate in Vermont make up the largest sector of the economy. Mining is the smallest. What factors might explain the difference in income of these two industries?

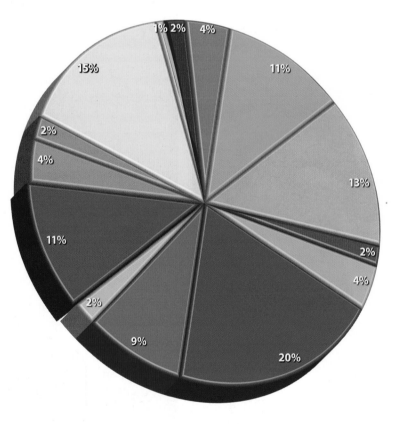

LEGEND

Agriculture, Forestry, and Fishing	$282
* Mining	$55
Utilities	$608
Construction	$883
Manufacturing	$2,863
Wholesale and Retail Trade	$3,131
Transportation	$510
Media and Entertainment	$909
Finance, Insurance, and Real Estate	$5,033
Professional and Technical Services	$2,152
Education	$611
Health Care	$2,706
Hotels and Restaurants	$1,099
Other Services	$625
Government	$3,653
TOTAL	**$25,120**

*Less than 1%. Percentages may not add to 100 because of rounding.

The production of electrical and electronic equipment, such as **semiconductors**, is among Vermont's leading manufacturing activities. IBM, one of the world's largest electronics companies, has a large plant in Essex Junction, near Burlington. IBM has operated in Vermont since 1957, and it is the state's leading employer.

Other modern manufacturing enterprises include the production of jet aircraft engines in the Rutland area and large-scale machinery in the Springfield and Windsor regions. Food processing, metal fabrication, and printing and publishing are also part of the economy in Vermont. The greatest portion of the state's earnings, however, comes from service industries such as health care, education, and tourism.

Green Mountain Coffee Roasters is one of the country's leading specialty coffee companies. Founded in 1981 in Waitsfield, the company now roasts its coffee beans in Waterbury.

Sheep were introduced to Vermont in 1811, and by 1840, the state had about six times as many sheep as people. When wool prices dropped in the mid-1800s, sheep farming declined and dairy farming increased.

Fabricated-metal products, including machine tools and precision metal parts, are among the state's top manufactured items.

Vermont's agricultural products include corn, eggs, greenhouse crops, and trees. Many Christmas trees from Vermont are sold on the streets of New York City in December.

Goods and Services

Many people would find a pancake incomplete if two of Vermont's key food products, butter and maple syrup, were not included. With farms occupying more than one-fifth of the land, agriculture is a vital industry in Vermont. Dairying has always been Vermont's main agricultural activity, and the state is a major producer of milk, butter, and other dairy products. Cattle, turkeys, sheep, chickens, and pigs are among the livestock raised in the state. Hay is grown to feed the dairy herds. Other agricultural products include potatoes, honey, and apples. In addition to maple syrup, Vermont is also a national leader in the production of maple sugar.

Transporting Vermont's goods within the state was not always simple. Many road improvements have made moving goods east-west through the Green Mountains much easier and safer. The Vermont Agency of Transportation continues to support and develop transportation networks that keep people and goods on the move.

Shelburne Farms produces specialty farmhouse cheeses. Workers make farmhouse cheddars, maple syrup, and hams using sustainable, humane farm practices.

Vermont has several notable private schools of higher education. Founded in the Champlain Valley in 1800, Middlebury is one of the oldest liberal arts colleges in the United States.

Services make up the fastest-growing sector of Vermont's economy. Tourism has been a major contributor to the development of the service sector. Millions of tourists visit the state each year, resulting in the creation and expansion of excellent resorts, hotels, restaurants, retail shops, and recreation facilities. Tourism also has been a driving force behind efforts to improve the state's roads and other transportation systems.

Vermont has been strongly committed to public education since colonial times. Its constitution of 1777 called for a state-supported university. The constitution also made it **mandatory** for each county to build an elementary school.

I DIDN'T KNOW THAT!

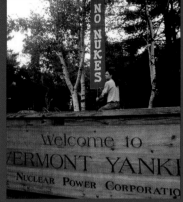

Vermont's only nuclear power plant produces about one-third of the state's electric power. In 2011, the Vermont Yankee power plant was granted a 20-year extension of its operating license. Opponents want to shut down the plant, citing safety concerns.

Farmers' markets and roadside stands throughout the state sell many of Vermont's locally produced goods.

Norwich University, in Northfield, is the oldest private military college in the United States. It was established in 1819.

There are about 190 public libraries in the state of Vermont.

The University of Vermont, in Burlington, was founded in 1791. It enrolls more than 10,000 undergraduate students.

American Indians

American Indians inhabited the Vermont region at least 7,500 years ago. Among those known to have lived there were a number of Algonquian-speaking groups, including the Abenaki, the Mahican, and the Penacook. These peoples relied heavily on the region's abundant natural resources and supported themselves with fishing and hunting. They hunted using snares and traps or bows and arrows. Each group consisted of small bands ruled by a chief, who advised the band members.

The Abenaki, whose name means "People of the First Light," were the largest group to occupy the Vermont area. **Archaeologists** have discovered evidence of Abenaki villages along the Connecticut River. Similar remains of Abenaki villages have also been found along Lake Champlain, near the mouth of the Winooski River.

American Indians of the Northeast created wooden snowshoes with leather webbing to help them move over the snow during winter hunts.

The Iroquois inhabited the Vermont region as well. This powerful group, originally from what is now the state of New York, invaded areas along Lake Champlain. The Iroquois managed to push many of the Algonquian groups out of the region long before any European explorers arrived. The Abenaki fought to defend their land from the Iroquois, and these two groups struggled for control of the area for many years.

Many Iroquois communities lived in fortified villages along the rivers and lakes of what is now Vermont. Their warriors wore face paint and jewelry.

The Abenaki called themselves Alnbanal, meaning "men."

Winooski is an Abenaki word meaning "wild onion." Wild onions once grew in abundance along the Winooski River.

Baggataway, or lacrosse, was a popular game among the Iroquois. Young American Indians play lacrosse today.

Explorers

T he first European known to have set foot in the Green Mountains was the French explorer Samuel de Champlain. He arrived in the Vermont area on July 4, 1609. He discovered a lake there that now bears his name. Champlain had left his encampment in Quebec so that he could join the Algonquian peoples in a battle against their enemies, the Iroquois. With the help of their new French allies, the Abenaki were able to regain control over much of the territory that they had lost to the Iroquois, including their land in the Vermont region. However, Champlain claimed the entire region for France.

The British also claimed Vermont. For about 150 years after Champlain's visit, the French fought with the British for control of the Vermont region and the rest of eastern North America. During this time very few Europeans explored or settled in Vermont, but the Lake Champlain region became a major battleground.

Samuel de Champlain, an early explorer of Vermont, was born in Brouage, France, in 1567. He made several voyages to North America during his career. In 1608, he founded Quebec, where he died in 1635.

Timeline of Settlement

Early Exploration and Settlements

1609 French explorer Samuel de Champlain discovers a lake now named after him in Vermont.

1666 The French establish a fort on Isle La Motte in Lake Champlain.

1690 British soldiers from the New York region build a fort at Chimney Point.

1724 A British fort called Fort Dummer, now a part of a state park, is built near Brattleboro.

British Rule and French and Indian War

1749 The royal governor of the British colony of New Hampshire begins giving colonists land in what is now Vermont.

1754–1763 France and Britain fight the French and Indian War, after which Britain gains control of Vermont and most of the rest of eastern North America.

1764 King George III of Great Britain rules that the New York colony has legal rights to the Vermont region.

1770 Frontiersman Ethan Allen organizes a force called the Green Mountain Boys to defend land that is now Vermont.

American Revolution

1775 During the first year of the American Revolution, Ethan Allen and his Green Mountain Boys capture Fort Ticonderoga from the British.

1777 Vermonters declare their region an independent republic, which lasts for 14 years.

1783 The American Revolution ends in the creation of the United States.

Independence and Statehood

1791 Vermont approves the U.S. Constitution on January 10 and becomes the 14th state to join the Union on March 4.

1793 A new state constitution is adopted.

Early Settlers

British colonists from Massachusetts established the first permanent European settlement in Vermont in 1724. Called Fort Dummer, it was located on the Connecticut River near the site of present-day Brattleboro.

Map of Settlements and Resources in Early Vermont

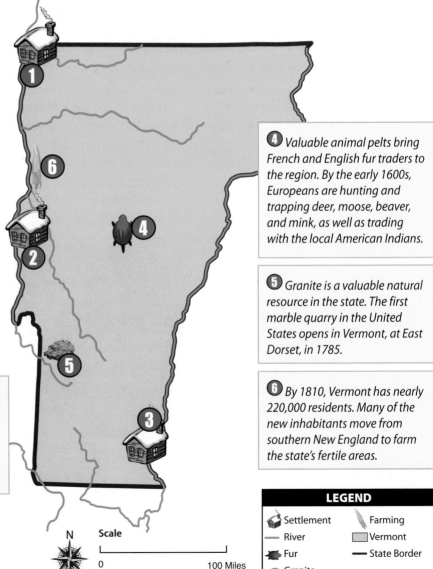

1 The French establish a fort in 1666 on an island in Lake Champlain.

2 English soldiers from the New York region build a fort at Chimney Point in 1690. This fort is used as a temporary outpost during the land struggles between France and Britain.

3 In 1724, British colonists settle in the Vermont region at Fort Dummer. Built of white pine trees, it is originally protected by some 40 British soldiers and 12 Mohawk Indians.

4 Valuable animal pelts bring French and English fur traders to the region. By the early 1600s, Europeans are hunting and trapping deer, moose, beaver, and mink, as well as trading with the local American Indians.

5 Granite is a valuable natural resource in the state. The first marble quarry in the United States opens in Vermont, at East Dorset, in 1785.

6 By 1810, Vermont has nearly 220,000 residents. Many of the new inhabitants move from southern New England to farm the state's fertile areas.

N

Scale

0   100 Miles

LEGEND

Settlement		Farming	
River		Vermont	
Fur		State Border	
Granite			

During the following years settlers from both New Hampshire and New York arrived in the Vermont area. Beginning in 1749 the royal governor of New Hampshire, Benning Wentworth, made grants of land, called the New Hampshire Grants, in what is now Vermont. New York also issued land grants, some of which were for the same land.

In 1764, the British king, George III, ruled that New York had **jurisdiction** over Vermont. Settlers who held New Hampshire Grants were soon ordered to surrender their land or pay New York for it. Armed conflicts between those who had rival claims became common. The Green Mountain Boys, under the leadership of soldier and frontiersman Ethan Allen, stopped sheriffs from enforcing New York laws and terrorized settlers who had New York grants.

Settlers in the region grew tired of the land disputes. On January 15, 1777, representatives of the towns in the New Hampshire Grants declared their region an independent republic. They named it New Connecticut. Six months later they renamed it Vermont.

The people of Vermont ran their independent republic for 14 years. The government of Vermont coined its own money, operated its own postal service, and **negotiated** with other states and countries. In 1790, New Hampshire agreed to give up its claim to Vermont. New York also gave up its claim that year after agreeing to accept $30,000 in compensation for New Yorkers who lost their land claims in Vermont. In 1791 Vermont became the 14th state to join the Union.

Vermont's population grew rapidly, and by 1810, the state had nearly 220,000 residents. By 1830, farmland no longer lured new settlers, but the growing manufacturing and mining industries were appealing.

American Indians in the area took sides during the battles between France and Great Britain for control of eastern North America. The Abenaki helped the French, while the Iroquois formed an alliance with the British.

The Champlain Canal opened in 1823. It connected Lake Champlain and the Hudson River in New York. The canal allowed Vermont farmers to ship goods to New York City, which was a major market.

There are more than 100 covered bridges in Vermont. The earliest ones date back to the 1820s and 1830s. The bridges were built with roofs and walls to protect the wooden **trusses** from decay.

Notable People

Many notable people from Vermont helped contribute to the development of the state and the country. They fought for independence from Great Britain, statehood for Vermont, and a fairer federal political system. The Green Mountain State produced two U.S. presidents as well as courageous military leaders, innovative manufacturers, educational reformers, and social activists.

**ETHAN ALLEN
(1738–1789)**

Ethan Allen was born in Connecticut in 1738. After fighting in the French and Indian War, he settled on territory, now in Vermont, claimed by both New York and New Hampshire. In 1770, Allen organized fighters known as the Green Mountain Boys to drive New Yorkers from the region. During the American Revolution, Allen and the Green Mountain Boys captured Fort Ticonderoga and Crown Point from the British. Ethan Allen died in 1789, two years before Vermont gained statehood.

**CHESTER A. ARTHUR
(1829–1886)**

The 21st U.S. president was born the son of a Baptist minister in North Fairfield in 1829. Arthur, a lawyer who had worked as fee collector for the port of New York, was elected vice president under James Garfield. He became president after an angry voter shot Garfield in 1881. As leader of the country, Arthur worked to end the practice of rewarding political supporters with jobs.

GEORGE DEWEY
(1837–1917)

Dewey, born in Montpelier in 1837, graduated from the U.S. Naval Academy. During the Spanish-American War in 1898, Dewey defeated the Spanish fleet at the battle of Manila Bay. The following year, the U.S. Congress created the rank of admiral of the navy for Dewey.

CALVIN COOLIDGE
(1872–1933)

Born in Plymouth, Vermont, Coolidge practiced law in Massachusetts and became governor of that state. A man of few words, "Silent Cal" was elected Warren Harding's vice president in 1920. After Harding's death in 1923, Coolidge was sworn in as the 30th president and served until 1929. Although successful during a prosperous time, Coolidge decided against running for reelection and died in 1933.

MADELEINE M. KUNIN
(1933–)

Born in Zurich, Switzerland, Kunin moved to the United States during World War II to escape the **Holocaust**. As a young woman, she worked as a newspaper reporter in Burlington. In 1985, Kunin became Vermont's first female governor. She was also the state's first Jewish governor.

I DIDN'T KNOW THAT!

Katherine Paterson (1932–), the popular children's author, was born in China and now lives in Barre. She has written many award-winning novels, including *Bridge to Terabithia* (1977) and *Jacob Have I Loved* (1981).

Ben Cohen (1951–) and Jerry Greenfield (1951–) started Ben & Jerry's, one of the country's most successful ice-cream companies, in a renovated Burlington gas station in 1978. The childhood friends from Brooklyn, New York, served their first scoop with a dream of "making the best possible ice cream in the nicest possible way." They combined producing premium ice cream in fun flavors with ecofriendly practices and social activism. They sold the company in 2000.

Population

Vermont is among the most rural states in the country. About three-fifths of the people live in villages or towns with fewer than 2,500 people. The rest of Vermonters live in the state's larger towns or cities, but even these urban centers are not highly populated. With more than 38,000 residents, Burlington is the largest city in Vermont. The state's second-largest city is Rutland.

Although Vermont's population is quite small, it has grown steadily since the mid–20th century, from about 400,000 in 1960 to more than 625,000 in 2010. Many new residents have moved from neighboring states to work in Vermont's high-technology industries.

Vermont Population 1950–2010

Between 1980 and 2010, Vermont's population grew by more than 20 percent. What factors might encourage or prevent that level of growth in the next 30 years?

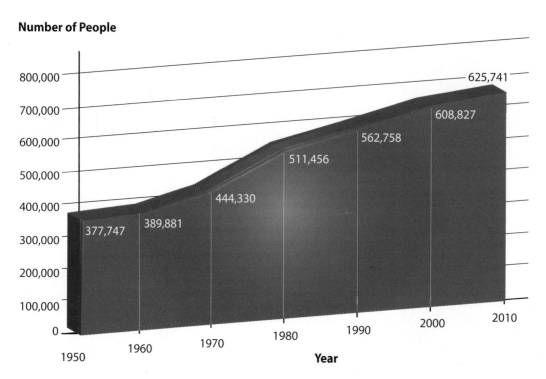

Number of People

- 377,747
- 389,881
- 444,330
- 511,456
- 562,758
- 608,827
- 625,741

Year: 1950, 1960, 1970, 1980, 1990, 2000, 2010

People of British descent make up the largest cultural group in Vermont. French Canadians are a sizable cultural group. Many people of French-Canadian heritage live in the Winooski area. People of Italian, Spanish, Welsh, and German descent also live in the state. In the 21st century, people from other countries continue to move to Vermont, but overall, fewer than 4 percent of the state's residents were born outside the United States.

There are 14 counties in Vermont. The most populated is Chittenden County. Five villages in Vermont have such small populations that they lost their official status as towns and no longer have local governments. They are Averill, Ferdinand, Glastenbury, Lewis, and Somerset. The largest of the five, Ferdinand, has a population of about 30 people.

Vermont is a rural state with a small population. Only Wyoming has fewer residents.

The most recent Vermont State House, located in Montpelier, took more than two years and $150,000 to build. It opened in 1859.

Politics and Government

Vermont's original constitution was established in 1777. It was the first constitution in the United States to ban slavery and allow all men the right to vote, regardless of income or property. Today the state is governed under its third constitution, written in 1793. It is the shortest state constitution in the country.

Vermont's state legislature is called the General Assembly. Its structure is bicameral, which means that it consists of two houses. One house is the Senate, which is made up of 30 members. The other is the House of Representatives, which has 150 members. Members of both houses of the General Assembly are elected to two-year terms.

The governor, who is also elected for a term of two years, is the head of the state's executive branch of government. Other elected members of the executive branch are the lieutenant governor, the attorney general, the secretary of state, and the treasurer. Vermont's highest court is the Supreme Court. It consists of a chief justice and four associate justices.

To the north of Vermont is the Canadian province of Quebec. The village of Derby Line marks the border on the pavement.

I DIDN'T KNOW THAT!

The state song of Vermont is called "These Green Mountains."

Here is an excerpt from the song:

*These green hills
  and silver waters
Are my home.
They belong to me.
And to all of her sons
  and daughters
May they be strong
  and forever free.*

*Let us live to protect
  her beauty
And look with pride
  on the golden dome.
They say home is
  where the heart is.
These green mountains
  are my home.
These green mountains
  are my home.*

Cultural Groups

People of many different ethnic backgrounds have made their homes in the Green Mountain State. The first people to live in what is now Vermont were American Indians. The first Europeans to establish a permanent settlement were Protestants of British heritage. They did so near what is now Brattleboro in 1724. In that same year Dutch settlers established a community in Pownal.

In the 1880s Vermont's granite industry, particularly in the Barre region, attracted skilled craftspeople and quarry workers from all over Europe. Italian and Scottish immigrants were among the largest groups to move to Barre. These groups worked to preserve many of the art forms and cultural traditions of their homelands. Some Scottish immigrants established a society called the Clan Gordon No. 12 of the Order of Scottish Clans. In all, immigrants from more than a dozen European countries moved to the Barre area to work in the granite industry.

Immigrant groups in Vermont's larger cities include Rwandans. Some of them give back to the community by helping out in schools.

Highland dancing, performed by Vermonters of Scottish descent at festivals, originated in Scotland.

Vermont's thriving textile industry also appealed to immigrants in the 1800s. French Canadians immigrated to the state to work in its textile mills. Many French Canadians settled in Winooski. Between 1850 and 1860 the French Canadian population in Winooski grew from about 3,000 to more than 4,300, and part of Winooski became known as French Village. Many of Vermont's French Canadians celebrate their distinct culture at Randolph's New World Festival.

Many of today's Vermonters are descendants of the state's early settlers. A variety of events are held across the state each year to celebrate the various cultures of Vermont's residents. For example, Stowe celebrates its German heritage with Oktoberfest. People of Scottish descent celebrate their heritage with the Quechee Scottish Festival. This festival features bagpiping competitions and Highland dancing. A stage showcases musical acts, such as fiddlers and **balladeers**. When attendees get hungry, they can sample some traditional Scottish food, including meat pies and **haggis**.

Some Abenaki still live in Vermont. They share their culture with visitors to the Shelburne Museum's annual Native American Intertribal **Powwow**. Representatives of other American Indian groups throughout the country also participate in this powwow, which features singing, dancing, and ancient rituals.

Along with Italian and Scottish immigrants, Barre attracted people from Lebanon, Spain, Norway, Denmark, Sweden, Finland, Greece, Serbia, and Poland in the late 1800s.

Vermont's minority groups are very small. African Americans, Asian Americans, and American Indians together make up less than 3 percent of the population. Hispanic Americans, who may be of any race, account for about 1.5 percent of Vermonters.

Arts and Entertainment

From bluegrass to jazz, music is popular in the Green Mountain State. Vermont is known for its many first-rate music schools. The Vermont Jazz Center, in Brattleboro, offers jazz classes, workshops, and concert performances. In the summer Marlboro College hosts the International Center for Advanced Musical Studies. Musicians from across the country head to the school to study chamber music. Marlboro's seven-week program ends with a music festival. Talented classical musicians from around the country travel to Vermont to teach and perform at the Killington Music Festival.

Among the many acclaimed writers and poets who have made their homes in Vermont over the years are Robert Frost, John Irving, David Mamet, and Jamaica Kincaid. Writer Sinclair Lewis lived in Vermont for a time. A memorial trail marked with his poems commemorates his time in the state.

Jamaica Kincaid, born in Antigua in 1949, spends summers in North Bennington. She wrote her first novel, Annie John, in 1985.

Born in New York City in 1894, Norman Rockwell moved to Arlington, Vermont, where he lived from 1939 until 1953. Rockwell featured many of the town's residents in his work.

Live theater is performed throughout the state. There are a number of playhouses that stage high-energy performances from local and visiting theater troupes. The Vermont Stage Company, based in Burlington, tours all over the state, performing in venues such as Burlington's Flynn Theater and the Barre Opera House. The Bread and Puppet Museum, housed in a 130-year-old barn in Glover, provides a unique experience for visitors. The museum features one of the world's largest collections of giant puppets. These puppets are brightly painted and crafted out of fabric and papier-mâché. In the summer the Bread and Puppet Theater presents a variety of puppetry performances.

The artist Norman Rockwell is best known for his depictions of American small-town life. The Norman Rockwell Exhibition in Arlington showcases many of his paintings. The exhibit is located in a 19th-century church. Sculptor Hiram Powers, famous for his statues of Benjamin Franklin, Thomas Jefferson, and Andrew Jackson, was born in Woodstock in 1805.

Sports

With clean air and unspoiled beauty, Vermont is a popular spot for outdoor activities. In the warmer months the Green Mountains welcome hikers and cyclists. Hikers are particularly drawn to Long Trail, which follows the crest of the Green Mountains for about 270 miles from the Vermont-Massachusetts border in the south all the way to the Canadian border in the north. Built between 1910 and 1930, it is the oldest long-distance hiking trail in the United States. The trail follows a challenging, rugged path through the mountains. Mountain biking is also popular on some Green Mountain National Forest trails. Vermont's many state parks offer other excellent hiking and cycling trails.

Water sports draw many visitors to Vermont. The state has more than 400 freshwater lakes and ponds. Lake Champlain features boating, and canoeing is popular on many of the mountain lakes. For experienced canoeists and kayakers, some stretches of the state's rivers offer great white-water challenges.

Mountain biking is a popular recreation in the Mountain State.

Skiing has long been the most popular sport in Vermont. In 1934 the first ski tow in the United States began operation near Woodstock. Since then many Alpine and cross-country ski resorts and centers have been established. Each winter skiers from all over the country flock to Vermont to enjoy its excellent ski facilities. Downhill ski areas in the state vary from steep, challenging runs to family-oriented hills. Among the downhill resorts are Killington, Mount Snow, Smugglers' Notch, Stowe, Stratton, and Sugarbush. Cross-country ski trails are located throughout the state. Snowboarding and snowshoeing are also popular.

Many of the best skiers in the United States have lived in Vermont. Exceptional Alpine skiers, such as Betsy Snite, Andrea Mead, Suzy Chaffee, and Billy Kidd, developed their talents on the Green Mountains. Bill Koch, a celebrated cross-country skier, is also from Vermont. In 1976, Koch became the first American to win an Olympic medal in Nordic skiing. Today many Olympic hopefuls gather in Vermont to compete in one or more of the state's ski competitions.

Killington, near Rutland, is the largest ski area in the eastern United States. The resort operates more than 20 lifts, including two gondolas.

I DIDN'T KNOW THAT!

Hannah Teter is an American snowboarder from Belmont. She won Olympic gold in the women's halfpipe in 2006 and silver in 2010.

Golf is a popular summer sport in Vermont. Among the state's most challenging golf courses are those at Stratton Mountain Country Club.

Vermont holds many winter sports events and competitions. Among the most popular are the Annual Fred Harris Memorial Ski Jumping Tournament in Brattleboro, first held in 1923, and the U.S. Open Snowboarding Championships in Stratton.

The Snowseum, at the base of Mount Snow, is a museum dedicated to the history of skiing in the United States.

Burlington has a minor league professional baseball team. The Lake Monsters play on Centennial Field, on the University of Vermont campus.

National Averages Comparison

T he United States is a federal republic, consisting of fifty states and the District of Columbia. Alaska and Hawai'i are the only non-contiguous, or non-touching, states in the nation. Today, the United States of America is the third-largest country in the world in population. The United States Census Bureau takes a census, or count of all the people, every ten years. It also regularly collects other kinds of data about the population and the economy. How does Vermont compare with the national average?

Comparison Chart

Statistic	USA	Vermont
Admission to Union	NA	March 4, 1791
Land Area (in square miles)	3,537,438.44	9,249.56
Population Total	308,745,538	625,741
Population Density (people per square mile)	87.28	67.65
Population Percentage Change (April 1, 2000, to April 1, 2010)	9.7%	2.8%
White Persons (percent)	72.4%	95.3%
Black Persons (percent)	12.6%	1.0%
American Indian and Alaska Native Persons (percent)	0.9%	0.4%
Asian Persons (percent)	4.8%	1.3%
Native Hawaiian and Other Pacific Islander Persons (percent)	0.2%	—
Some Other Race (percent)	6.2%	0.3%
Persons Reporting Two or More Races (percent)	2.9%	1.7%
Persons of Hispanic or Latino Origin (percent)	16.3%	1.5%
Not of Hispanic or Latino Origin (percent)	83.7%	98.5%
Median Household Income	$52,029	$52,111
Percentage of People Age 25 or Over Who Have Graduated from High School	80.4%	86.4%

*All figures are based on the 2010 United States Census, with the exception of the last two items.

How to Improve My Community

Strong communities make strong states. Think about what features are important in your community. What do you value? Education? Health? Forests? Safety? Beautiful spaces? Government works to help citizens create ideal living conditions that are fair to all by providing services in communities. Consider what changes you could make in your community. How would they improve your state as a whole? Using this concept web as a guide, write a report that outlines the features you think are most important in your community and what improvements could be made. A strong state needs strong communities.

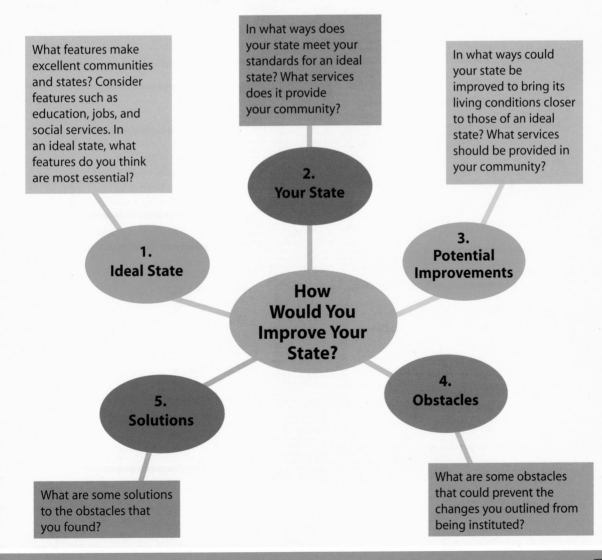

What features make excellent communities and states? Consider features such as education, jobs, and social services. In an ideal state, what features do you think are most essential?

In what ways does your state meet your standards for an ideal state? What services does it provide your community?

In what ways could your state be improved to bring its living conditions closer to those of an ideal state? What services should be provided in your community?

2. Your State

1. Ideal State

3. Potential Improvements

How Would You Improve Your State?

5. Solutions

4. Obstacles

What are some solutions to the obstacles that you found?

What are some obstacles that could prevent the changes you outlined from being instituted?

Exercise Your Mind!

Think about these questions and then use your research skills to find the answers and learn more fascinating facts about Vermont. A teacher, librarian, or parent may be able to help you locate the best sources to use in your research.

1 Who was the only president born on Independence Day (July 4)?

2 True or False? Vermont is home to the oldest log cabin in the United States.

3 Vermont's first railroad was named for what two cities?

4 Which of the following was Vermonter Thomas Davenport responsible for inventing?

a. The electric railway
b. The electric motor
c. The electric printing press
d. All of the above

5 True or False? The first postage stamp used in the United States was made in Vermont.

6 True or False: Many Vermonters believe that there are sea monsters in Lake Champlain and Lake Memphremagog.

7 What famous admiral and hero of the Spanish-American War was born in Vermont?

8 Vermonter James Wilson is credited with creating:

a. The first camera made in the United States
b. The first globe made in the United States
c. The first answering machine made in the United States
d. The first wristwatch made in the United States

Words to Know

archaeologists: scientists who study early peoples through artifacts and remains

balladeers: singers of folk songs

conifers: evergreen trees with needles and cones that keep their needles all winter

deciduous: trees and shrubs that shed leaves every year

glaciers: large bodies of ice that move very slowly

haggis: a traditional Scottish pudding made of the heart, liver, and lungs of a sheep or a calf, which is boiled, along with vegetables and oatmeal, in the animal's stomach lining

Holocaust: the mass killing of European Jews and others by the Nazis during World War II

jurisdiction: legal control over a region

mandatory: made into law, compulsory

migratory: moving seasonally in search of food and shelter

negotiated: discussed, dealt, or bargained with another or others

nitrogen: a gaseous element that makes up about four-fifths of Earth's atmosphere and is also found in animals and plants

powwow: an American Indian ceremony

quarries: large pits from which stone is extracted

semiconductors: basic electronic components used in computers and communications equipment

textile: relating to cloth

trusses: frames designed to support bridges

Index

Log on to www.av2books.com

AV² by Weigl brings you media enhanced books that support active learning. Go to www.av2books.com, and enter the special code found on page 2 of this book. You will gain access to enriched and enhanced content that supplements and complements this book. Content includes video, audio, web links, quizzes, a slide show, and activities.

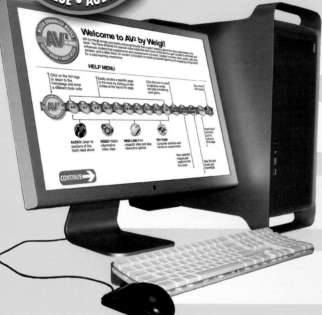

Audio
Listen to sections of the book read aloud.

Video
Watch informative video clips.

Embedded Weblinks
Gain additional information for research.

Try This!
Complete activities and hands-on experiments.

WHAT'S ONLINE?

Try This!	Embedded Weblinks	Video	EXTRA FEATURES
Test your knowledge of the state in a mapping activity.	Discover more attractions in Vermont.	Watch a video introduction to Vermont.	**Audio** Listen to sections of the book read aloud.
Find out more about precipitation in your city.	Learn more about the history of the state.	Watch a video about the features of the state.	
Plan what attractions you would like to visit in the state.	Learn the full lyrics of the state song.		**Key Words** Study vocabulary, and complete a matching word activity.
Learn more about the early natural resources of the state.			
Write a biography about a notable resident of Vermont.			**Slide Show** View images and captions, and prepare a presentation.
Complete an educational census activity.			**Quizzes** Test your knowledge.

AV² was built to bridge the gap between print and digital. We encourage you to tell us what you like and what you want to see in the future.
Sign up to be an AV² Ambassador at www.av2books.com/ambassador.